MW01154963

"I would beg to disagree, but begging disagrees with me"

– FIONA APPLE, *UNDER THE TABLE*

© Publication: Penguin Random House South Africa (Pty) Ltd,
The Estuaries No 4, Oxbow Crescent, Century Avenue, Century City, 7441
PO Box 1144, Cape Town, 8000. Oh, hullo. You don't have to read this bit – it's not a part of the story
and there are no important questions here. Promise.

www.penguinrandomhouse.co.za

© Text: Deshan Tennekoon 2021

© Illustrations, layout and design: Linki Brand 2021

Publisher: Nandi Lessing-Venter

Proofread by: Glenda Laity

Set in Adobe Garamond Pro

Printed by ABC Press

First edition 2021

978 0 6396 0829 7 (printed book)
978 0 6396 0836 5 (ePub)

Mary Anning's
GREWSOME
BEASTS

DESHAN TENNEKOON AND LINKI BRAND

SCOTLAND
NORTHERN IRELAND
IRELAND
ENGLAND
WALES
LONDON
LYME REGIS
JURASSIC COAST

CONTENTS

DEAR READER,

It is not easy to tell the story of someone as
brain-bogglingly brilliant as Mary Anning.

It makes a writer nervous – from the very start of the book,
they must show Mary's courage and grit; her cunning detective skill;
her contribution to science.

It ought to be a serious and thoughtful book.
Unfortunately, this one involves squirrel jokes, umbrellas and poop.

Our story is set around about 200 years ago (but not around a roundabout, since they hadn't been invented yet). We will call Mary's time the 'Olden Days'. These are a different kind of olden days to the 'Seriously Olden Days'. We will encounter these later, when we meet Mary's grewsome beasts. We may also learn why 'grewsome' is spelled like that.

In the Olden Days, no one had electricity in their homes. Instead, light came from candles made of cow, pig or sheep fat (the *original* scented candles). Sometimes, light came from setting fire to gooey fluid in glass lamps (whale oil, usually). All of these methods wheezed horrid smoke.

The Olden Days were days when a man's moustache looked as if a semi-dead squirrel had been nailed to his lips. A time when

happens in the grim, grey winters of an English beach town named Lyme Regis. 'Lyme Regis' means 'flood of the King' and that tells you a lot about the sort of place it is in winter.

women dressed as if someone had opened a beach umbrella beneath their skirts. It was a frightening time to be a fashionable adult.

In this book, we will meet Mary's parents and her brother, Joseph. We will meet her friends, the people she worked with and also, her very nice dog.

And what about the poor children, you ask? The poor children all had jobs; the rich ones had education. The Olden Days were a terrible time to be a poor child (a bit like today).

In addition, the following will appear in our story –

This brings us to Mary Anning. When our story starts, she is a baby, and when our story ends, she will be dead.

 A fast cart stacked with heavy rocks

 Tall, murderous waves

 Hands with too many bones

 A (mostly) rock-proof hat

Adding to this not-very-cheery atmosphere, quite a lot of our story

 200-million-year-old poo

Haunting this whole tale, are a clutch of clever but selfish men, some of whom own large, twitchy (and possibly itchy) moustaches. Mary will do her very best to get the better of them.

Our story also takes place in the Jurassic period (200 million years ago) – The Seriously Olden Days. If you were in Mary's town in the Jurassic period, you'd be deep underwater but at least the water would be bright and tropical.

The sea around you would be full of life – strange beings curling and weaving their way past; little things darting and glinting; huge things gliding down below in the deep dark.

Millions of years after they died, Mary found some of these creatures. The land that would one day be Lyme Regis had preserved them.

When animals die in the ocean, their bodies sink to the seafloor (unless they're gobbled up on the way down). Sand and mud from the land wash into the sea and settle on the bottom, like a blanket for the dead. Slowly, slowly, the bones of the dead absorb minerals from the sand and mud and sea, and turn to stone. These stony remains are then called 'fossils'.

Millions of years later, that ancient seafloor of Lyme Regis had risen high above the ocean. Today, you can find clues to that older world, hidden in the rocks of the coast.

One last thing before we begin. This book will show you only six of the fossils that Mary found. Partly, because Mary found too many fossils for a book as slim as this,

and partly because the scientists of her day did not often name the *finder* of a fossil – only the person who *described* it to other scientists. The six fossils in the book are extremely weird in exciting ways, so it's not all bad news.

And now it's time to meet Mary and to uncover a hidden history of the world, pulled from the stone by her muscle and mind.

This illustration is based on *Duria Antiquor* by Henry De La Beche (a geologist and good friend of Mary's) who aimed to celebrate her greatest discoveries through this visual representation

BABY VERSUS LIGHTNING

The first year of your life is generally quite nice. You ride a friendly giant to get where you're going; your underpants are handmade each day; you know only two restaurants, but both are excellent.

Mary Anning was born on the 21st of May 1799. In her first year, the sky tried to kill her.

When she was one year old, on an August day under a sky the colour of cobwebs, Mary was taken to meet some horses. (We don't know how she felt about this because she was one year old and no one knows what one-year-olds think about horses.)

What should have been a day in a nice field, meeting herbivores as tall as doors, turned out to be very nasty indeed, because on this day came a towering storm. To hide from the bucketing rain, Mary, her nanny and two teenagers huddled under an elm tree. Lightning lunged from the clouds, struck the elm and killed three of the four people under it.

At first, everyone was sure Mary had died, too. She lay cold and still on the soaking grass. She was taken away; lowered into a warm bath. Fingers were crossed; prayers were said.

The world, as they say, held its breath.

Someone should have told the world not to worry. Even as a baby, Mary Anning was a fighter. No mere lightning strike was going to end her life. In the battle of Baby –vs– Lightning, there would be only one victor. The people of Lyme Regis were amazed but Mary had only *started* being amazing.

'VERTEBERRIES' AND WHY YOU SHOULDN'T EAT THEM

Mary's lovely beach town, Lyme Regis, drew tourists like flocks of well-dressed seagulls. When Mary was four, one such tourist – a famous and excellent writer named Jane Austen – visited the town and met Mary's dad. She wanted a broken pitcher mended at his shop. We do not know what Mary felt about this, as we do not know what four-year-olds feel about brilliant writers or busted jugs.

When she was old enough, Mary went to Sunday School and learned to read and write and be Christian, but that was all the schooling she got. Mary's family were poor, but Mary was determined – all through her life she taught herself what she thought she ought to know, and she was wise enough to learn from clever friends.

Mary's father, Richard, was a cabinetmaker. This did not bring the family enough money, so he also collected and sold fossils to tourists. In the Olden Days, fossils were called 'curies' or 'verteberries' or 'snakestones' or 'devil's fingers' (the word 'fossil' was still new and maybe no one liked it much – although they didn't mind calling people who collected fossils, 'fossilers').

Tourists saw verteberries and bought verteberries but didn't think much about them. To the people of Mary's time, they were simply odd stones and bits of bone. There were two important ideas you and I take for granted that people in the early 1800s had not fully grasped.

One was that the Earth was a *lot* older than religion said it was. Religion told them the planet was thousands of years old. It was unthinkable that Earth might be *billions* of years old.

The other idea was that the animals living here today had not always been here – there had been other animals in the past and something had killed them all.

Without these two bits of knowing, it was hard for people in Mary's time to understand how important those verteberries were. Those two ideas – that we now call 'deep time' and 'extinction' – began to take hold in Mary's lifetime and her work helped prove both of them. Extinction, in particular, made some religious people angry – were geologists saying God made mistakes and erased animals? At the same time, it made other religious people happy – they thought, Aha! Maybe these were animals Noah didn't load on his ark! It was a confusing time to be religious and an exciting time to be a scientist.

Mary received her first geologist's hammer from her father. Mary and her brother, Joseph, helped their dad when he went collecting the 'verteberries' that fell from the cliffs they called the Blue Lias (this means 'blue-grey limestone'). The best time to do this was in the biting embrace of winter, because in the hammering rain and screaming wind, the cliffs would slide and tumble to the sea, which meant new fossils turned up. Mary loved it when

this happened – it was like the Earth gave her gifts each time it rained.

But going to the cliffs was dangerous – everyone knew this. One day the cliffs may give you a fossil, the next day they may take your life. But if you were a fossil hunter, you went anyway.

When she was 11, Mary's father fell from the tall, blue cliffs. He survived the fall but his injuries, along with an illness, stole him from Mary soon after. Following his death, Mary's mother now had to work twice as hard to look after the children as well as Richard's small fossil shop.

Joseph took over their father's cabinetmaking job. But however much they worked, money was hard to earn. One winter, they were so poor they sold their furniture to pay the rent. Their church gave them food when it could, but the early years after Richard's death were difficult. And every day, Mary had to work the same unfeeling cliffs that took her father from her.

THREE WARS AND A LITTLE ICE AGE

The French Revolution ended in the year Mary was born but the French Revolutionary Wars were only starting. The Anglo-Spanish War was raging, too; it was a dangerous time to live in Europe. One reason there were so many tourists in Mary's town was because it was risky to travel outside your own country and you had to holiday where you could.

To make things stranger, Mary was born near the end of the Little Ice Age (1300-1850). It wasn't the sort of Ice Age with mammoths rumbling about, but it *was* cold enough to freeze Europe's rivers*. It even froze the Baltic Sea! In China, it grew too cold to grow oranges (bad news – oranges are excellent). In Africa, snow on the mountains came close to the ground and there was flooding everywhere. In South America, there were icebergs in lakes and lagoons!

*In London, the River Thames froze solid enough for markets and parties on the ice (like that episode of Doctor Who when Bill and the Doctor visit the 1814 frost fair but there's something under the ice eating children and...*what do you mean you don't watch Doctor Who?!*)

THE FIRST
GREWSOME
BEAST

Hunting fossils one day, Joseph discovered a strange, enormous skull.
It looked a bit like a crocodile skull or maybe that of a fish. But it had holes
as big as dinner plates in its head. Some guessed the holes were for the beast's
eyes (they were right), but no one was sure what kind of creature it was.

Mary was 12 at the time. She decided to find the rest of the skeleton,
which is a perfectly sensible thing for any 12-year-old to do when
they see a dead monster. For nearly a year she dug, mindful of the
high, icy waves hurtling up the beach to strike hard the tall, grey
cliffs. Many times, the waves tried pulling her out to sea.

Mary's beast from the beach was a beautiful mystery. When the fossil was
dug free of the rock, she had the pieces taken to her home in a huge cart.
After days of cleaning and brushing and looking and thinking, Mary drew
its skeleton, carefully counting each strange bone. No one knew it yet, but
she had found a reptile from the ancient sea called an *ICHTHYOSAUR!*

Ichthyosaur means 'fish lizard,' except no one had given it this name yet, so in the meantime they called it a 'grewsome beast' (spellings from The Olden Days were weird).

Ichthyosaurs were air-breathing animals like you and I, but they had mouths full of deadly, pointed teeth and a bite more powerful than almost anything they met in the sea. In place of hands, they had paddles and the paddles were very unlike your hands. Human hands have four fingers and a thumb. Each finger has three bones (your thumb has two). Some kinds of ichthyosaur had up to nine 'fingers' and as many as 30 bones in each finger! That's the most number of hand bones of any animal, alive or dead.

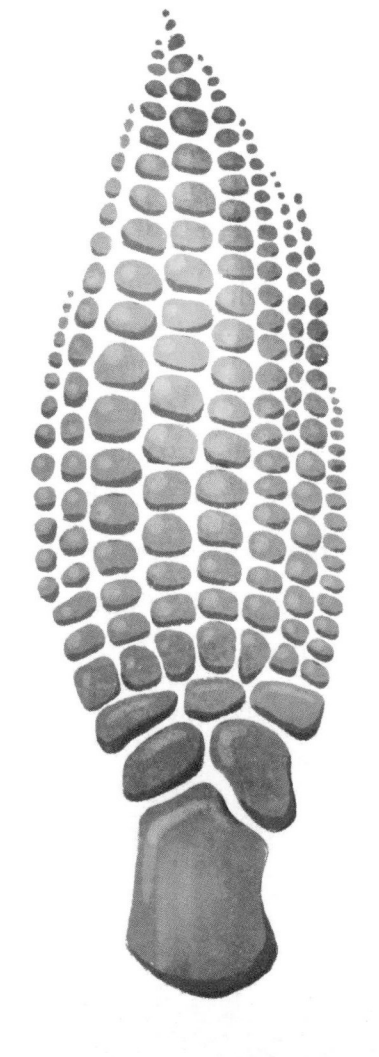

There were many kinds of ichthyosaurs, and the one Mary found was called *Temnodontosaurus platyodon. Temnodontosaurus* means 'cutting-tooth lizard' and *platyodon* means 'broad tooth.' It lived about 200 million years ago in the Early Jurassic and was the first of its kind ever found.

Temnodontosaurus platyodon was one of the most fearsome marine predators of its time, seeking prey in dark waters with its enormous eyes (the largest of any ichthyosaur). We now know these high-speed hunters were happy eating fish, but they were also fond of gobbling up smaller ichthyosaurs (which seems an icky thing to do).

Like her father would have, Mary sold the ichthyosaur to a fossil collector and an idea sparked in her head. If she could find more grewsome beasts and her mother could sell them, maybe they could make a life for themselves. And why not? She was good at finding things, good at seeing in the rock secrets that no one else could see.

Even after it had gone to the fossil collector, Mary dreamed of the beast. She wondered about the ancient, mystifying creature – what had it looked like when it was alive? Did it have babies or lay eggs? Did it swim alone or with its family?

It would be a long time before anyone knew, but we do now, so the answers are:

- the picture on the next page is a pretty good guess
- it had swimmy, bitey babies born straight into the water
- we think it might have hung out (and hunted) in groups

It lived 200 million
years ago in the

**EARLY
JURASSIC**

FISH?

CROCODILE?

Eyes as big as dinner plates!!!

**ICHTHYO-
SAUR**

means
'FISH LIZARD'

Mary (12)
decided
to find the
rest of the
skeleton

Mary's brother,
Joseph, discovered
the skull

Temnodontosaurus had the **BIGGEST EYES** of any animal we've measured

TEMNODONTOSAURUS means cutting-tooth lizard

Ichthyosaurus poo

ik-thee-uh-saw

ICHTHYOSAUR!

The one that Mary found was of the Temnodontosaurus kind

Now we know that their babies were born straight into the water!

Did it look like this when it was alive? It is estimated that some grew as large as **12 METRES (39 FT)!**

AN UGLY TRUTH ABOUT MARY'S WORLD

The Dorset coast, where Mary hunted fossils, could be a dangerous place. The beach Mary trod each day was thick with fallen geology and even the tides far out at sea were not to be trifled with. When she was 16, a sailing ship returning from India sank off the coast and drowned bodies washed up on the shore.

On her beach, Mary found one of the corpses. She cleaned seaweed from the dead woman's hair and had it taken to the church. Until the dead woman's family arrived to claim the body, Mary visited every day to leave fresh flowers on the body.

Time passed.

Mary grew older, got herself a black and white dog and made some friends.

One of these friends was Elizabeth Philpot, a fellow fossil hunter who had moved to Mary's town some years earlier. Elizabeth was an expert at fossil fish and explored the beaches often with Mary.

Then there was Henry De La Beche, who moved to Lyme Regis when he was a boy. He made friends with Mary and fell in love with fossils. Henry grew into a clever geologist and a good painter.

But there is an ugly fact about Henry we must remember – although he respected Mary and helped her many times, he also owned a plantation in Jamaica with 200 slaves. He said he wanted to improve the lives of the slaves, but he kept the plantation for many years.

The Olden Days are full of stories like this. The British Empire, for instance, would continue to own slaves until around 1844 and, like Henry, the lady we meet next also came from a family that owned slaves. So did the husband of another of Mary's friends, Charlotte Murchison. Facts like these can make the world seem a hopeless, cruel place if people as kind as Henry can *at the same time* be part of something as horrific and brutal as slavery. The world is different now, but we mustn't forget what it used to be.

BOULDERS TOPPLING, BIG AS BUILDINGS

Another friend of Mary's was Anna Maria Pinney, daughter of a wealthy slave-owning businessman. In her journals, Anna Maria writes of long talks with Mary about fossils and religion (and tells the story of the shipwreck, too). She also writes of a lady in Lyme Regis called Mrs. Stock, who gave a young Mary Anning her first book on geology. Many of the things we know about Mary come from Anna Maria's journals. Always keep a journal – a historian might need it in the future.

Anna Maria walked with Mary under the unpredictable cliffs, but she was terrible at spotting when the sea was trying to kill her. We will meet her again in a paragraph or two, but first we must meet Mary's black and white terrier, whom she called Tray.

Tray was named after either:

a) The dog of a mad king named Lear in a play by Mister Shakespeare, or

b) A flat container for carrying biscuits, milk, sugar *and* a cup of tea in a single hand, while gripping this book with the other. Brilliant things, trays.

Tray travelled with Mary as she hunted grewsome beasts hidden in the cliffs. Of the many hours they spent, more than many were dangerous. The sea near the cliffs where the best beasts were found always grew savage after a storm. Mary once had to save Anna Maria (the Pinney from earlier) from tall, icy waves that nearly crushed them both – at the last second, before the wave broke, Mary hoisted up Anna Maria and heaved her to safety.

The cliffs never stopped trying to kill Mary. Chunky clumps of rock – some as big as hippos – would leap from the top and crash on the beach below. And since the cliffs were as high as they were, even small rocks could kill. Once, one of these small rocks – about the size of a goat – fell to the beach and very nearly killed Mary.

Who knew beaches could be so deadly? And if you were a woman doing this work, there was another problem. Having read this far, you won't be surprised to learn that people who say things like, "Girls can't climb cliffs!" and "Girls need indoor hobbies!" wagged their fingers and said exactly those things. But did Mary listen? There are three possibilities:

1. No, she didn't,
2. She picked up her sturdy hat,
3. Put on her sturdy hat ...
4. and went straight to work.

The numbers speak for themselves.

Before we go along to meet more weird reptiles, we must pause to study Mary's very fine hat. Mary wore a top hat to work, and this may seem odd since her office was a beach. But she was using an old geologist's trick. You take a top hat, which is made of stiff wool and you coat it with a sticky fluid called 'shellac'. Shellac comes from female Lac bugs in Asia and the liquid turns rock hard when it dries. Geologists in Mary's time would coat their top hats in shellac and turn them into tall, tough helmets. Pebbles falling from the cliffs above would politely *boing* off your hat, leaving your head undented.

Let's pause here so you can ask a parent to please buy you a top hat and a jar of Lac bugs.

THE SECOND GREWSOME BEAST

If you thought life got a little easier for Mary, now that she'd found a
rare fossil that baffled science, you should be congratulated on the size
of your optimism. As fossil hunters, Mary's family enjoyed some small
fame, but fame can't buy fish or fruit and hunger won't sleep and winter
wears knives. And while Mary's life was often grey, with darker patches
still to come, there were, every now and then, rare dots of colour.

One of these rare dots was Lieutenant-Colonel Thomas James Birch. Birch
was a geologist and fossil collector who bought many fossils from the Annings.
He believed that almost all the best fossils science knew of had been found
by Mary. On hearing Mary's family had money troubles, he sold
off his entire collection and gave Mary's mother the money. The
family was safe from hunger for a short while.

In case the 'short while' turned out to be more 'short' than 'while', Mary
worked even harder. She hunted among the jumbled rocks by the sea,
searching for gifts from the storm. In 1821, she found a good one –
a fossil in excellent condition, from a species of ichthyosaur that would
be named *Ichthyosaurus communis* (communis means 'common').

Life loped along.

With one eye on the grasping waves and crumbling cliffs, Mary scoured the beach by day, returning home at dusk, shivering and tired. Some evenings, armed with a scalpel, she peered into fish or unzipped squid. She made neat notes about the things she learned about modern animals and thought about how they related to extinct ones. On other evenings, working by oil lamp, she copied out long scientific articles borrowed from friends so she could read them later and learn from them. Mary Anning was always busy.

When she was 24 years old, Mary found a second grewsome beast no one had seen before. She dug and brushed and cleaned for weeks, and when she finished, she had found the first complete skeleton of an ancient reptile that would one day be called a **PLESIOSAUR**.

Plesiosaur means 'near to lizard', which is a dull name to give an animal who looks as if a snake, a turtle and a giant almond had a baby together.

These improbable beasts had a bizarre number of neck bones. You and I have seven neck bones. Plesiosaurs could have up to 70!

The shape of their bodies and the way they moved made them unique among all Earth's creatures, living or extinct. Millions of years ago, in all the world's oceans, plesiosaurs swam gracefully with a strange, bird-like flapping of their four, long paddles. Like their necks, these paddles also had a bizarre number of bones. Plesiosaurs had up to 8 'fingers' in each paddle, and each 'finger' could have up to 18 bones.

Their teeth were like heavy needles and they ate fish, clams and belemnites (we'll meet them later). Like ichthyosaurs, these grewsome beasts gave birth to live young and we think they may have lived in groups. Plesiosaurs ruled the seas for 180 million years – the longest that any meat-eating ocean reptile has ever ruled.

These are facts we know today. Back in Mary's time, people had trouble believing plesiosaurs were real. The ones with moustaches said things like 'This grewsome beast is a fake!'

Even Georges Cuvier, a famous French scientist (who did not have a moustache and therefore should have been more sensible) said the animal's neck was too long to be a real neck. This was terrible news for Mary – people would surely believe Cuvier, who was a man and rich and a baron and a famous scientist. People thought of him as 'the father of palaeontology', the new science Mary was helping to create.

Cuvier was as respected as the sea and as well-known as the onion – Mary had even taught herself French to read his brilliant scientific papers. You won't be surprised to learn that people believed him instead of Mary. But those who had bought Mary's fossils or worked with her, those who knew how clever and thoughtful and honest she was, believed she had found a true and real grewsome beast. Two geologists in particular, stood by Mary – Henry De La Beche (who we met earlier) and William Conybeare. They fought to convince the men of the cities that Mary's beast was not a fake.

HENRY DE LA BECHE
We believe Mary has found a true and real grewsome beast!
WILLIAM CONYBEARE
This is the FIRST complete Plesiosaurus EVER FOUND!
Its neck is too long to be a REAL neck ...
GEORGE CUVIER
HUMAN NECK (7 BONES)
PLESIOSAUR NECK (UP TO 70 BONES)
PLESIOSAUR
plee-see-uh-saw
Plesiosaurs had smooth skin, letting them glide swiftly through the sea

These paddles helped them swim gracefully underwater

Some scholars thought the fossil was so fantastical that **IT WAS FAKE!**

They gave birth to live young

They ate fish, clams and belemnites

It is estimated that some grew as large as **10 METRES (33 FT)**

The shape of their bodies and the way they moved make them unique among all Earth's creatures

And so the men of science, in far London and Paris argued over Mary's grewsome beast with the excitingly long neck. They did not invite Mary to speak – remember, this story happens in the Olden Days when men did some truly, blindingly stupid things, like not allowing women to do science.

After much manful shouting, moustache wrenching and a thumping of perfectly innocent desks, Cuvier and the others admitted their mistake. The men of science agreed that Mary's new beast was real after all.

Mary, of course, knew this all along. They named Mary's plesiosaur *Plesiosaurus dolichodeirus* (the last part means 'long neck'). It still hangs in the Natural History Museum in London today.

INVISIBLE SCIENTISTS
These are some women working during Mary's lifetime as geologists (mostly):

Etheldred Benett GEOLOGY / PALAEONTOLOGY

Mary Buckland GEOLOGY/ PALAEONTOLOGY /SCIENTIFIC ILLUSTRATION

Arabella Buckley GEOLOGY

Elizabeth Cobbold PALAEONTOLOGY/BOTANY

Lady Eliza Maria Gordon-Cumming PALAEONTOLOGY /HORTICULTURE/SCIENTIFIC ILLUSTRATION

Maria Graham GEOLOGY

Barbara Hastings GEOLOGY

Delvalle Lowry GEOLOGY

Mary Elizabeth Lyell GEOLOGY/ PALAEONTOLOGY - FOSSIL SHELL EXPERT

Mary Ann Mantell GEOLOGY/ PALAEONTOLOGY /SCIENTIFIC ILLUSTRATION IGUANADON TEETH DISCOVERY

Charlotte Murchison GEOLOGY/PALAEONTOLOGY/SCIENTIFIC ILLUSTRATION

The Philpot sisters (Elizabeth, Mary and Margaret) GEOLOGY/ PALAEONTOLOGY

Mary Somerville MATHEMATICS/ASTRONOMY/GEOLOGY

MARY SOMERVILLE

SHE SELLS FOSSILS AT HER OWN FOSSIL SHOP

In 1825, Mary met a brilliant scientist whom no one realised was a brilliant scientist because she was a brilliant woman scientist. Her name was Charlotte Murchison. Charlotte was a geologist and scientific illustrator. She met Mary on a visit to Lyme Regis and became her friend. This was especially good news for Charlotte's husband, the famous geologist, Roderick Impey Murchison, who benefitted from Mary's deep knowledge and sharp mind.

By this time in her life, Mary had saved enough money to buy a tall, thin shop. She named it 'Anning's Fossil Depot'. 'Depot' is a clever word to use. It means a place where you store 'large quantities of equipment, food or goods'. In naming her shop that way, Mary was saying, "I have *loads* of stuff to sell." And sell she did.

SHE DOES NOT SELL SEASHELLS BY THE SEASHORE

'She sells seashells by the seashore' is a famous English tongue twister. Some people think it is about Mary, but there's no evidence for this – not even a tiny bit. This is sad because it's a good tongue twister, but Mary would have wanted proof before she twisted her tongue, and we should too.

The shop was where Mary and her mother would live and work. Mary would find the fossils, and her mum would manage the business.

Mary's father would have been proud. Tray was probably proud too, but we are not certain of this because no one knows what small dogs think about tall, thin shops.

A few years later, Mary visited Charlotte in London. Charlotte took Mary to the Geological Society of London and the British Museum. Many of Mary's fossils hung on the walls, her name nowhere to be seen.

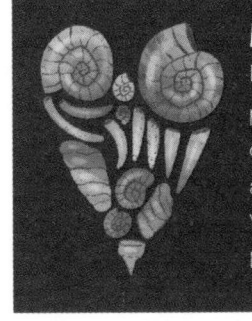

MARY IN LOVE

Did Mary fall in love? Was there someone who made her heart go pitter-pat? Mary didn't leave many writings of her own and Anna Maria doesn't say anything in her journals about Mary's crushes. There are books and films that say maybe Mary loved Charlotte or Henry or one of the Williams (Conybeare). Did she? We don't know. If Mary ever was in love, did the someone she loved return her love? We can only hope.

THE THIRD AND FOURTH GREWSOME BEASTS

Mary and her friend Elizabeth Philpot (and Elizabeth's sisters, Margaret and Mary) spent all seasons hunting fossils.

The Philpot sisters were wealthy enough that if they wanted to, they could keep any fossil they found – and they found many. One reason geologists visited Lyme Regis in Mary's time was Mary; the other reason was the large and neatly labelled 'Philpot Collection'. If you find yourself in England and you can trot to Oxford, you can still see the Philpot Collection in the Oxford University Museum of Natural History.

Mary was less lucky than the Philpots; she had to sell most of the fossils she found and Anning's Fossil Depot sold fossils of all sorts. Among them were prehistoric sea creatures called ammonites and belemnites.

AMMONITE

Ammonites are named after a symbol called 'the horns of Ammon'. Ammon was the name of an Egyptian god, often shown wearing ram's horns on his head. Belemnites get their name from the Greek word for 'dart' or 'arrow', 'belemnon', which is a good choice given how odd their bodies were.

Ammonites and belemnites were squiddy-looking animals, but not the soft, squiddy animals you get today, like the octopus, cuttlefish or squid. Some had shells that curled in on themselves (the ammonites); others had pointy, cone-shaped bodies and pointy, cone-shaped skeletons (the belemnites). Belemnites, you'll remember, were a healthy snack for plesiosaurs, while ammonites were on the menu for many a shark and ichthyosaur.

BELEMNITE

Tourists visiting Lyme Regis loved belemnites and ammonites, and Mary sold many. Both kinds of beast lived in large numbers in the ancient seas. Their fossils were not hard to find along the coast and the Annings were always busy. Molly tended the tourists and Mary was away at the cliffs in the salted wind, hunting and hoping.

Then one day, she met a truly odd fish.

In a four-line story, a newspaper from 1828 tells us of a nearly perfect fossil found by Mary. Imagine a fish shaped like a pancake with a tiny mouth and powerful, grinding teeth. It would be named **DAPEDIUM POLITUM** and it lived in the same seas as ichthyosaurs and plesiosaurs. *Dapedium politum's* sturdy teeth let it pulverise shellfish for lunch (and probably dinner and maybe breakfast, too).

Teeny, tiny mouth but

POWERFUL, GRINDING TEETH!!!

"Miss Anning, of Lyme, has found a large perfect specimen of the *Dapedium Politum*, an antediluvuan fish, with oblong scales. This specimen is unrivalled."

1 DECEMBER 1828
SALISBURY AND WINCHESTER JOURNAL

THE SALISBURY AND WINCHESTER JOURNAL

Some grew as large as **30CM** (about a foot)

Its head was armoured and its body scales were as tough as your teeth!

DAPEDIUM POLITUM

da-pe-de-um po-lih-tum

1828 was to be a good year for Anning's Fossil Depot. Mary and Tray walked the beach every winter, spring, summer and autumn (but mostly winter), and when she was 29 years old, Mary found an astonishing fossil. This one would make our world richer and deeper, like her ichthyosaur and plesiosaur discoveries did. But unlike those fossils, this grewsome beast was not a swimmer. When it was alive, long ago, it sailed the skies on leathery wings and sang songs we'll never know.

The slim, hollow bones of this tiny grewsome beast were as fragile as a fashion model who has skipped breakfast for a month. Each of its hands (the beast's, not the model's) had one finger as long as two pencils. Mary dug and brushed and cleaned more carefully than ever, and when she was done, she discovered a reptile that would be named **DIMORPHODON MACRONYX.**

'Dimorphodon' means 'two-form tooth', and 'macronyx' means 'large claw.' This tells us the animal had two kinds of teeth and large claws (sometimes, scientific names are awfully direct). Having two kinds of teeth is weird for a reptile, so maybe it was proud of the fact while flying the Jurassic skies, some 200 million years ago.

Dimorphodon macronyx was a tiny, ancient pterosaur. *Pterosaur* means 'winged-lizard'. Pterosaurs are special because they were one of the first animals with a backbone, to fly. Until they evolved, insects ruled the skies of Earth. Mary found most of the fossil. Her friend Elizabeth discovered its sharp teeth, of which there were far too many for comfort.

About 174 years after she dug it from the rock, we are still learning about Mary's pterosaur. By studying its legs and claws and teeth, we think it could climb trees to eat insects and small lizards. It's a strange little beast – we don't yet know where it fits on the pterosaur family tree, but we do know it was one of the first of its kind. If you wrote a history of pterosaurs, Dimorphodon would be in Chapter One.

Mary's *Dimorphodon macronyx* was the first pterosaur found in Britain and the third pterosaur ever found by human beings.

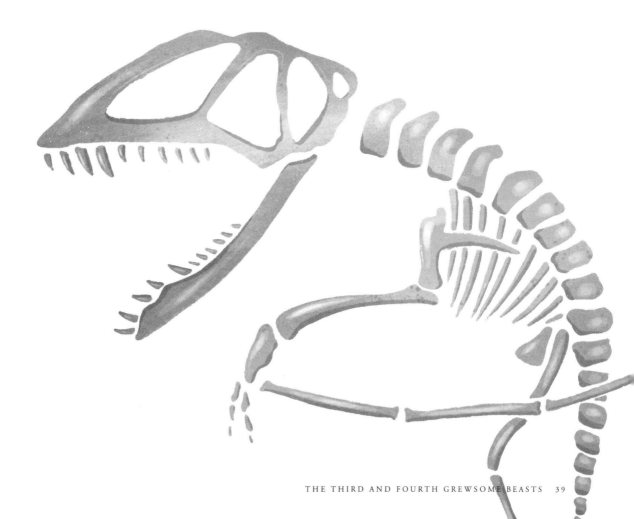

Dimorphodon had **2** kinds of teeth

They were one of the

FIRST

animals to fly!

We think they were able to climb trees

It is estimated that some grew as large as

1 METRE (3.3 FT)
with a wingspan of
1.45 METRES (4.6 FT)

Mary had discovered the first pterosaur to be found in Britain

Elizabeth Philpot discovered its sharp teeth

Dimorphodon macronyx is a
PTEROSAUR
meaning 'winged lizard'

DIMORPHODON

MACRONYX

di-morf-o-don
ma-kron-ix

A STRANGE PLACE TO GET YOUR ART SUPPLIES

In the same year she found her *Dapedium* and *Dimorphodon*, Mary discovered that belemnites had ink sacs inside them, like squid do today. Even better, Elizabeth found if she scraped off the powdery ink and added water, it turned into ink again, after millions and millions of years – imagine the joy of that discovery! Best of all, you could draw with it! You only got one colour though – brown. Elizabeth drew with it and posted a detailed picture of an ichthyosaur skull to her friend, the geologist Mary Buckland.

Mary Buckland's husband, William was also a famous geologist. He was one of the few scientists of the time who would credit the women he worked with. Buckland wrote a scientific paper about Mary's discovery, and soon, everyone wanted to paint with ink older than humanity.

NEVER
BREAKFAST
WITH BUCKLAND

We must pause now to learn what snacks William Buckland liked. It's not important to Mary's story, but every now and then, it's good to take a strange detour.

A warning: this will get ghastly fast, so hop ahead if you like.

William Buckland decided to eat every animal on Earth. Or, at least, he wanted to try one from each species. You might think a church leader had better things to do, but Buckland, like *Dapedium*, was an odd fish. Here are some animals he ate and enjoyed: bear, crocodile, dog, hedgehog, horse, ostrich, porpoise, and turtle. He was particularly fond of mice on toast. Animals he ate and did *not* enjoy: bluebottle flies and moles.

There is a story (we're not sure how true) that while at a dinner party, Buckland was shown the tiny, embalmed heart of King Louis XIV and he promptly ate it. We should stop here – who knows where this road leads?

Actually, we *do* know where it leads – it leads straight to Buckland's son, Francis, who had equally bizarre eating habits, but there is no time now. We must return to Mary, whose contribution to science cost us fewer turtles and taught us more than a Buckland Breakfast.

SUSPICIOUS STONES AND A FIFTH GREWSOME BEAST

In 1829, the hairy-lipped men of science began to study something Mary had known for years – that some of the spotted 'stones' on the beach were exactly like the spotted 'stones' found inside grewsome beasts (in the tummy and backside regions).

They were not stones at all.
They were, in fact, fossilised poop.

These poop-stones are called 'coprolites' and they are good to study if you want to know what grewsome beasts ate. Scientists in Mary's time did not use the word 'poop', but then, they wouldn't let Mary join their science club, so what did they know?

While the men prodded poo from the dawn of time, Mary was busy unearthing another peculiar, grewsome beast. This one was an ancient fish. It looked as if a shark, a manta ray and a chainsaw had a baby together. Mary dug and cleaned and brushed and discovered an animal that would be called **SQUALORAJA POLYSPONDYLA.**

Squaloraja means 'shark ray' and *polyspondyla* means 'many vertebrae'. When Mary sent the men of science her *Squaloraja* fossil, at first they were confused. Some saw it and thought 'lizard!' Others thought 'bird!' Some agreed with Mary (fish!) but they thought it was a modern fish. Mary, who spent years comparing modern beasts to ancient ones, agreed it looked a *bit* like modern sharks or rays, but she suggested it was much, much older.

The men of science argued for four years and didn't invite Mary to take part even once. In the end, as they did with her plesiosaur, they realised Mary was right. What she had found was a completely unknown creature – a 200-million-year-old animal that showed a connection between sharks and rays. Mary's discovery was an important link in the great evolutionary chain of Earth.

The fossil of poor old *Squaloraja* met a sad end, though. Along with some of Mary's ichthyosaur and plesiosaur fossils, most of the *Squaloraja* fossil was destroyed in World War II, when the museum in Bristol where they stayed was caught in the bombing.

After her discovery of *Squaloraja*, Mary's fame as a brilliant fossilist grew, but so did the number of new fossil hunters.

SQUALORAJA POLYSPONDYLA

skwo-luh-raa-juh po-li-spon-di-luh

This went on for four years!

Definitely FISH

FISH!

BIRD!

LIZARD!

It is estimated that some grew as large as 60CM (2FT)

Part of the fossil Mary found was destroyed when the museum in Bristol was bombed during World War II

It was a link between sharks and rays

The beaches were crowded and Mary worked harder than ever to find fossils, but not long afterward, her family was in need of money. Luckily, her old friend Henry De La Beche had a solution.

Henry made an action-packed painting of grewsome beasts from Dorset, featuring many of the animals Mary discovered. He sold prints of the painting and gave the money to Mary and Molly. The original painting featured a magnificent, pooping plesiosaur (see page 9). People of Mary's time thought it rude to show poop in a painting, so you can still find copies with the poop removed (but why would you want that?).

Life improved a little and one year later, Mary discovered the fossil of a new kind of plesiosaur that was named *Plesiosaurus macrocephalus* (*macrocephalus* means 'big head'). She also dug up as a lovely ichthyosaur fossil (probably *Ichthyosaurus communis*). Mary sold them both so she could keep working.

Now it is time to draw near your box of tissues or tub of handkerchiefs (do handkerchiefs come in tubs? No one knows – it's a mystery). If they're in another room, now is the time to fetch them...

THE SIXTH GREWSOME BEAST

If you have never been under a cliff, watching a landslide (and if you have, you are most likely dead and not reading this book at all), here is how one can happen: First, you need a storm. Days of hard rain and wind loosen the rock and soil at the top of a cliff. Huge waves driven by the storm smash and weaken the base of the cliff.

Next, parts of the weakened clifftop begin to dance. Great big, clumping lumps of earth – some larger than elephants – lunge into the open air and crash down on the land below, creating a slope. Stone and mud and sand and trees slide and smash their way to the ground.

Then all is quiet… save for the whispering earth on the beach below as waves crush the fallen cliff into smaller clumps. You may think the worst is over but it is, of course, not. The rocks and soil on the cliff above are still slewing and sliding down to the ground. There are many rocks, some the size of buffalos, some the size of teenage baboons, and they are all racing to reach the beach below.

When Mary was 34, a landslide like the one above (and coming from the same direction) nearly killed Mary and entirely killed Tray. Mary's friend had been standing a few feet from her, when the Earth fell and took him away.

Mary never had another dog.

On her way to work on a December morning that same year, while it was still early enough to be dark, a heavy cart carrying rocks from a quarry smashed into Mary. It pinned her body to a rough wall of stone. Its weight nearly crushed her. The driver and some passing townsfolk heaved the cart away, and Mary escaped with no serious wounds. Mary, of course, still went to work that day.

Some years later, in 1839, Mary found a rare, complete fossil of a new grewsome beast. It looked as if someone had glued two small spears to a medium-sized shark. This ancient fish might be the oldest creature Mary ever found. It would be named *HYBODUS DELABECHEII*. We'll come back to that familiar-looking second name – the name of its species – in a minute.

Hybodus means 'hump tooth', which sounds like an insult worth remembering ("Get lost, hump-tooth!"). It was a prehistoric shark the length of a coffin with strange spikes on its back that we think might have been used for defence.

Because you are a sensible human being, you may think the person who finds a fossil is the person they name the fossil after. But the world is not so fair, certainly not in Mary's time (and also not now, sorry). The man who gave Mary's *Hybodus* its species name, chose to honour a famous local geologist (Henry) instead of the discoverer (Mary). We shouldn't be shocked but we should be cross.

It had two kinds of
teeth, so it could catch
slippery snacks (fish)
and crunchy snacks
(animals with shells)

Named after
Henry De La Beche

HyBODUS
DELABECHEII

Some ancient sharks
were older than
even the dinosaurs!

It is estimated that
some grew as large as
**2 METRES
(6.6 FT)**

hai-boh-dis de-la-beech

We think the strange spines on
its back might have been used
for defence

ANNINGIA

IN MARY'S NAME

Here are some fossils named for Mary. Most of them were named long after she died.

FISH (species) – *Acrodus anningiae* (1841) and *Belenostomus anningiae* (1844): Two of the very few species named after Mary during her lifetime. Both were named by Louis Agassiz, a clever Swiss palaeontologist with whom Mary often talked about work.

CORAL (genus and species) – *Tricycloseris anningi* (1878) Named by R.F. Tomes.

MAMMAL-LIKE REPTILE (genus) – *Anningia* (1927) Named by Robert Broom.

BIVALVE MOLLUSC (genus) – *Anningella* (it was called Anningia in 1936 by L.R. Cox but changed to Anningella to avoid confusing it with another fossil by that name).

SEED SHRIMP (species) – *Cytherelloidea anningi* (1974) Named by Alan Lord.

PLESIOSAUR (genus) – *Anningasaura* (2012) Named by Peggy Vincent and Roger B. J. Benson.

ICHTHYOSAUR (species) – *Ichthyosaurus anningae* (2015) This fossil was found in the 1980s, mistaken for a copy made of plaster and used as a teaching aid. It was rediscovered in 2008 by a sharp-eyed 18-year-old named Dean Lomax. In 2015, after studying it and realising it was a new species, Dr. Lomax and Prof. Judy Massare named it after Mary.

SLIPPERY LAND,
A SAXON KING AND
THE FATE OF MOLLY ANNING

1839 was a big year for the tall, thin shop where Mary and
her mother lived and worked – and a big year for geology,
too. But it was the start of dark days for Mary.

That year, William Conybeare had two guests for Christmas –
Mary Buckland and her William (he of the mouse-on-toast breakfast).
In the night, an enormous landslide shook the area. Conybeare and
the Bucklands rushed to investigate. We do not know if dramatic
music played in their heads during the carriage ride over.

Conybeare and the Bucklands had always wanted to learn why
landslides happened, and here was a chance to study one happening.
They walked all around the landslide, trying to see it from every
angle. Mary Buckland made careful, detailed scientific drawings;
the two Williams wrote down their theories, and the book they
published became the first scientific study of a major landslide.

We don't know if Mary visited the landslide. It happened nearby in
a place called Binden – about 3 miles from Lyme Regis. Maybe the
way Tray was killed haunted her still and Mary didn't go; maybe she
went, but since no one (including Mary) wrote about it we can't tell.

But we do know Mary had a difficult time of it, that year.

Anning's Fossil Depot was selling lots of fossils but Mary's mother, Molly, had grown ill. Mary would continue to hunt fossils, conduct research, run the shop and also look after her mum. Time passed in this way for a slow while. In 1842, after working her entire life; losing eight children; losing her husband; raising Mary and Joseph by herself and running a busy shop – Molly Anning died.

For the first time, Mary was alone in the house – with her fossils and her work and now, her own growing illness – a cancer in her breast.

Time ground onward.

A fire burned through Lyme Regis in 1844, destroying homes and shops. Anning's Fossil Depot was lucky to survive. In July that year, Mary received a visit from a king (no moustache) and the king's doctor (moustache ownership uncertain). They came from the Kingdom of Saxony (a small slice of Germany with some quite nice grapes) to visit the famous Fossil Depot.

The king's doctor bought an ichthyosaur fossil to add to the king's collection. Mary was mildly annoyed, and rightly so, to learn they did not know who she was. She crisply informed the doctor of her name, and that she was known across Europe as an expert fossilist. We can only hope the king and the doctor were suitably ashamed and bought a few more fossils.

And now, here we are at the darkest part of this book. It's the part where we part with Mary Anning. We saw her grow from a lightning-fighting baby into a young girl who dug monsters from the rock; we watched her question and study and become a woman who changed science. We clenched our fists as she was ignored and doubted; we grinned when she was proved right.

But here, now, is the end of Mary's time
and the end of our time with her...

MARY ANNING OF THE GREWSOME BEASTS

Mary's cancer grew inside her. So did pain.

She found it hard, then harder, then impossible
to continue her work at the cliffs.

She was given powerful medicines, but they could not heal her because,
in Mary's time, doctors could not completely treat breast cancer
(we still don't have foolproof ways). Some of the medicines dulled the
pain but made her groggy and forgetful. People started saying awful
things about her; that she was a drunk; that she was lost to the world.

The Geological Society of London raised money for her;
her friends and colleagues helped when they could. Mary was
able to pay her rent and live, but it was no kind of living.

She kept working in the shop until,
on the 9th of March 1847, just before
her 48th birthday, Mary Anning died.

She was buried a few days later at
St. Michael's, her local church.

The world had lost a brilliant scientist. Mary's fossils enriched the theory of extinction; her work with coprolites helped us understand whole ecosystems lost to time. Even the idea that once there was an 'age of reptiles' was helped along by Mary's discoveries.

In the strange anatomy of 'grewsome beasts', Mary Anning had been an expert. Her work helped make a brand new science called palaeontology. She was a finder, a thinker, an artist, and friend. Mary Anning did not bend to winter storms, deadly seas, collapsing cliffs or foolish men. She helped us discover the world as it was in the faraway past, and in doing this, Mary Anning changed the future.

IN MARY'S MEMORY

When Mary died, the flow of extraordinary fossils from Lyme Regis dwindled. The moustached men of science came to realise whom they had lost. Henry De La Beche spoke of this in the obituary he wrote for Mary. A few years later, Henry and the two Williams (Buckland and Conybeare) had the Geological Society of London install a stained glass window in Mary's honour at St. Michael's church in Lyme Regis. (It's still there and you can go see it.) Two official portraits of Mary were commissioned, too. If you've ever seen a portrait of Mary, chances are it's one of those.

How can we honour such a remarkable human?
How do we keep her memory alive?

One way to remember Mary Anning is by using the arts. Whether you like making drawings or puppets or digital models; dances, plays or songs; kites or clothes or cardboard sculptures – if we make some noise about the good humans, maybe more humans will want to be good. It can't hurt to try...

Another way is to join in the life of your town. Have you heard of the project to erect a statue of Mary in Lyme Regis? It was started by Evie Swire when she was 11 years old, with help from her mum, Anya Pearson. Since there was no statue of Mary in town, Evie began a change in the world by saying to the people in charge that there *ought* to be a statue. With a persistence Mary Anning would have liked, Evie convinced them. One day soon, a statue of bronze by a sculptor named Denise Dutton, will stand in Lyme Regis.

Maybe in the end, the best way to honour Mary is to grow up determined, clever and kind. Never wait to be taught; find what you love and learn it on your own, if you have to. Offer help when it's needed. And when they make fun of you, when they bully or laugh or push you down – speak truth, put on a stiff hat and go back to doing what lifts you up.

Good luck to us all!

END.

Illustration based on Dutton's maquette of Mary and Tray

ACKNOWLEDGEMENTS

DESHAN IS GRATEFUL FOR:

Tracy, Neha and Khavan; you are the world around which I make my wobbly way. I love you. Vajira and Yasmin; I am grateful to be your child and that you showed me a path to be a good human. (It's hard though, no?) Soharni, Youssef, and their hummingbird-marshmallow, Maya. Hiya, Maya! Want a hammer and top hat?

Shehan Karunatilaka and Ruwanthie de Chickera; for hard truths and encouraging words. Aftab Aziz; for his years of patience in the face of my endless, foolish questions. Leslee Udwin; for having me write stories for Think Equal, and Cait Robertson, for being a kind, quick-witted companion.
Dr. Andrew Kittle, Anjali Watson, Ayla and Amara; for reading my stories and always finding ways to make them better.

Dr. Anjana Khatwa, Dr. Dean Lomax and (soon-to-be-doctor) Natalia Jagielska; for kindly allowing me to rummage about their brains. I hope I didn't leave any crisp packets behind. Professor Hugh Torrens; for his scholarly work on Mary Anning and for entertaining the questions of a whippersnapper. Professor Larry E. Davis; for his many papers on Mary Anning and her world.

My editor, Nandi; who championed this book and wove all its threads together. Linki; whose sheer grit made it possible, and whose art makes it shine.

For saving me from the jaws of Hybodus, Squaloraja and Dapedium – The Palaeontological Association, Emma Bernard and the NHM Fossil Fish Section of the Natural History Museum of London, Jake Atterby, Dr. Sam Giles, Dr. Tony Timlin, and Dr. Dennis Hansen. To the fine people of Twitter who graciously answered my questions about women scientists of the early 1800s. I'm sorry I couldn't include them all.

And finally, to the crows who visit me for breakfast; I love you, but please stop pecking my books – there's no dinosaur food inside.

LINKI IS GRATEFUL FOR:

Deshan; for his brilliant sense of curiosity and wonder and tender approach to the world. Nandi; for your trust and comradery in more than one way. Werner, Fia, Ben and little Lukas for your never-ending love and support. And finally; my parents, Nerina and Jan; for giving me the space to draw with all sorts of things on all sorts of things.

WHO MADE THIS BOOK AND HOW TO PUNISH THEM

DESHAN TENNEKOON wrote it. He hates cashews and naps. To punish him, send him cashews and tell him to take a long nap. That'll show him. When he is not avoiding naps or punting cashews into the sun, Deshan writes storybooks, non-fiction books (like this one) and comics. He also takes photographs and designs books. Deshan lives in Sri Lanka – a warm little island with tall hills.

LINKI BRAND made the pictures and fitted them together with the words, to create a book. Since she did (at least) two jobs, you may need to punish her (at least) twice. She hates travelling and horror movies. To punish her, you can buy her a plane ticket and then scare her in the airport. Linki makes pictures and designs books, but always at weird times of the day. She lives in Norway; a long country with gneiss rocks and crisp air.

NANDI LESSING-VENTER edited this book. She absolutely hates chocolates. To punish her, post her a large chocolate egg. Nandi is secretly a penguin. Everyone she works with is a penguin. That penguin logo on the book isn't just a nice picture of a dinosaur. Nandi lives in South Africa; the country with the largest asteroid impact crater in the world.

GLENDA LAITY is the proofreader of this book. She's had to work really hard, really fast and doesn't deserve punishment. If she hadn't been apart of our teem, these book mite have luked like a reel mess, ewe no?

ABC PRESS printed and bound the book. They take Linki's digital files and print them onto huge sheets of paper – many pages of our book fit on one sheet of a printer's paper. Then they fold and cut it and glue it to the cover to make a book.

THE PRODUCTION TEAM does many jobs. They make sure the book is made quickly and well; they send copies of the book to bookshops and digital books to online shops; they advertise the book so readers know about it. This is a lot of work for penguins and they are only paid in fish.